ART · FROM · THE · PAST

The
GREEKS

GILLIAN CHAPMAN

Heinemann
LIBRARY

GENERAL CRAFT TIPS AND SAFETY PRECAUTIONS

Read the instructions carefully first, then collect together everything you need before you start work.

It helps to plan your design out first on rough paper.

If you are working with papier mâché or paint, cover the work surfaces with newspaper.

Always use a cutting mat when cutting with a craft knife and ask an adult to help if you are using sharp tools.

Keep paint and glue brushes separate and always wash them out after use. Use non-toxic paints and glue.

Don't be impatient – make sure plaster is set, and papier mâché and paint are thoroughly dry before moving on to the next stage!

All projects make perfect presents! Try to make them as carefully as you can.

RECYCLING

Start collecting materials for craftwork. Save newspaper, clean coloured paper and card, cardboard boxes and tubes of different sizes, glossy paper and gift wrap, and scraps of string and ribbon.

Clean plastic containers and old utensils are perfect for mixing plaster and making paper pulp.

PICTURE CREDITS

AKG Photos: /Erich Lessing 6 bottom left, 36, /John Hios 6 bottom right: **British Museum:** 20, 22, 32, 34; **C M Dixon:** 7 top left; **Michael Holford:** 7 bottom left, 8 top right, 8 bottom right, 8 bottom left, 10, 12, 14, 16, 18, 26; **Piraeus Museum, Athens:** 24; **Robert Harding:** 7 bottom right; **Science Photo Library:** /John Sanford & David Parker 28; **Sonia Halliday Photographs:** /F H C Birch 30.

ART FROM THE PAST: THE GREEKS was produced by Fernleigh Books, 61A Southbury Road, Enfield, Middlesex, EN1 1PJ.

Designers: Gillian Chapman and Gail Rose
Photographer: Rupert Horrox
Illustrator: Teri Gower Picture Researcher: Jennie Karrach

First published in Great Britain in 1998 by Heinemann Library, an imprint of Heinemann Educational Publishers, Halley Court, Jordan Hill, Oxford OX2 8EJ, a division of Reed Educational and Professional Publishing Ltd.

Heinemann is a registered trademark of Reed Educational & Professional Publishing Limited.

OXFORD PORTSMOUTH NH (USA) CHICAGO
SINGAPORE MELBOURNE AUCKLAND KUALA LUMPUR
IBADAN GABORONE JOHANNESBURG KAMPALA NAIROBI

© Fernleigh Books 1998

British Library Cataloguing in Publication Data
The Greeks. - (Art from the past)
1.Handicraft - Juvenile literature 2.Art, Greek - Juvenile literature 3.Imitation in art - Juvenile literature
I.Title
745.5'0938

ISBN 0 431 08065 8 (Hardback)   ISBN 0 431 08067 4 (Paperback)

Printed in Italy.

The author and Fernleigh would like to thank Keith Chapman for all his help with the model making.

ART · FROM · THE · PAST

The GREEKS

GILLIAN CHAPMAN

THE GREEK EMPIRE

THE LAND OF ANCIENT GREECE was made up of a hot, mountainous **peninsula**, surrounded by hundreds of small islands. Small isolated communities grew up all over this area, often cut off from each other by sea or mountains. These small communities grew into the Greek states, which consisted of a city supported by the surrounding countryside. Each independent state had its own laws and government.

Although the states, such as Athens and Sparta, were constantly quarrelling amongst themselves, they were all united as Greeks. They all spoke the same language, worshipped the same gods and shared the same customs. They became a strong united force when they fought a common enemy, such as the victorious war against the Persians.

LEFT. *The city of Ephesus, in Asia Minor, had a huge sanctuary dedicated to Artemis, the Greek goddess of hunting.*

BELOW. **Athens** *was the most powerful city state and the Athenians built temples to their gods on the* **Acropolis***.*

Law, Order and Knowledge

The idea of a **democratic** government was a Greek concept. The first democracy was established in Athens in 508 BC. The Greeks enjoyed an ordered society in which individuals had great freedom and power. Creative thinking and personal achievements were encouraged. They admired the complete man – someone who was equally talented as an athlete, a poet or a philosopher.

The Greeks excelled in many scientific areas, such as astronomy, mathematics and **philosophy**, which is the love of knowledge. They were a sea-faring nation and needed the knowledge of astronomy for navigation. Greek architects relied on laws of geometry and mathematics for their engineering and building. Their styles of architecture have influenced many cultures that have followed after them.

ABOVE. **Aristotle** (384–322 BC) had a great love of knowledge. He was a politician, poet, scientist and philosopher.

LEFT. *The treasury of the Athenians at Delphi.*

BELOW. *Fallen column drums at Athens show how the huge columns were constructed in sections.*

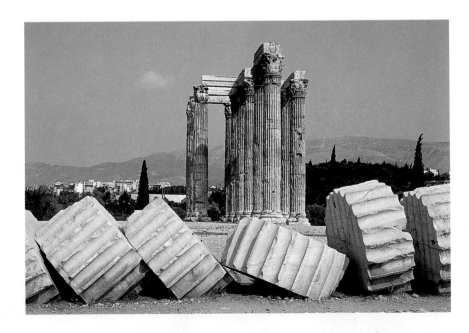

ARTS AND CRAFTS

THE GREEK LOVE OF BEAUTY shows itself in their art and architecture. Sculpture was created in honour of the gods and was displayed in temples and public buildings. It showed a perfect view of life – men with strong healthy bodies, beautiful women draped in fine clothes, and strong horses carrying brave warriors. Skilled sculptors and artisans worked for patrons that demanded very high standards.

Poets were also held in high esteem and the language of poetry, often set to music, developed into the high forms of literature and theatre which are still greatly admired today. Ancient legends and poems were memorised and passed on by storytellers. The most famous legends were written down by Homer in the *Iliad* and the *Odyssey*, and historians now believe that many of these epic tales are based on fact.

RIGHT. *A caryatid figure from the Erechtheum, the temple of Athena on the **Acropolis** at **Athens**.*

BELOW LEFT. *The 4th century BC theatre at Delphi.*

BELOW RIGHT. *Vase painting of the legends of Homer.*

GREEK CRAFT TIPS

Painting and finishing projects is exciting. It is the most difficult part, so take your time. By following these simple painting tips everyone will be happy with the results.

Paint the masks in a dark colour and leave to dry. Brush a lighter colour on, leaving some of the dark paint showing through. Finally brush with gold paint to get a special effect.

Build up layers of different coloured paint to achieve brilliant effects. Keep the brush dry and use the paint sparingly. Don't draw in all the details if you don't want to!

Greek craftsmen were clever, but not at everything! Vases were made by a potter, but painted by an artist. When you paint pictures on a project, draw out the design first.

Don't be afraid to rub out or start again. Only trace onto the project when the design looks right. Fix the tracing paper with tape to stop it moving while you are tracing down.

The Greeks believed that if something was worth doing, it was worth doing well. In this same spirit, try to make your projects as carefully as you can.

9

DOLPHIN FRESCOE

THE WALLS OF MANY TEMPLES and palaces were once decorated with beautiful **frescoes**. Originally these scenes were painted directly into the wet plaster. However, over the centuries they have become damaged and many have been restored by modern artists, copying fragments of the original paintings.

There are many remains at the **Minoan** royal palace on Knossos, an island of **Crete**. This fresco decorates the walls of the Queen's apartment.

The ancient Greek world was made up of the mainland of Greece, with its rugged coastline and many islands. Dolphins were often sighted in the warm coastal waters.

DOLPHIN FRESCO

YOU WILL NEED

Cardboard	Newspaper
Paper & pencil	String & scissors
Tracing paper	Poster paints
Ruler & sticky tape	Fine paint brush
Cutting mat	Plaster, an old container
Craft knife	& mixing utensils

1. Work out your design on rough paper following the ideas shown here. Copy the dolphins and the border patterns on the fresco.

2. Measure the design and make a cardboard mould the same size, with sides 5 cm deep. Score the sides, turn them up and tape together.

3. Mix up the plaster in an old container, following the instructions on the packet. Pour the plaster into the mould to a depth of 3 cm.

4. Smooth the surface of the plaster. Cut a 15 cm length of string and push the ends into the wet plaster, leaving a loop to hang the fresco up when it is dry.

5. When the plaster is dry carefully remove it from the mould. Trace down your dolphin design onto the smooth surface and pencil in the outlines.

6. Following the pencil outlines, carefully colour in the dolphin design using poster paints and a fine brush. Try copying the colour scheme of the original fresco (far left).

LABYRINTHS

THE ANCIENT GREEK LEGEND of the Minotaur tells of a monster – half man, half bull – who lived in the **labyrinth** on the island of Crete. Each year children were sacrificed to the monster until Theseus, the prince of Athens, decided to go to **Crete** to try and stop the killing.

The labyrinth was so complicated, no one had ever returned, but Theseus used a ball of string to mark his way. He bravely killed the Minotaur and used the string to retrace his steps.

The legend of **Theseus** killing the Minotaur was painted on this Greek vase in 450 BC.

ROLLING BALL PUZZLE

YOU WILL NEED

Shallow box with lid	Glue stick
Craft knife & cutting mat	Paints or felt pens
Cardboard	Paper scraps
Scissors	Coloured marbles
Paper & pencil	String

1. Design your puzzle so it is the same size as the bottom of the box. Incorporate into the design several places where the marbles must rest.

2. Cut out a piece of cardboard the same size as the design. Mark on the card where the marbles will rest and cut the holes out neatly.

3. Carefully glue the card into the bottom of the box and leave to dry. Then draw the puzzle design onto the card with paints or felt pens.

4. Colour the box and lid with poster paints or felt pens, or decorate it with the coloured paper scraps.

5. Try making a maze by gluing a coil of string into a box. Paint the string when the glue is dry and try guiding the marbles through the maze. How many can you get in the centre of the spiral?

Make it more difficult to roll marbles into the holes of the Minotaur puzzle by making the holes smaller and shallower.

When you are not playing with the maze or puzzle, replace the lid to keep the marbles safe!

13

TEMPLE COLUMNS

THE GREEKS BUILT magnificent temples to honour their gods. They used only the finest materials and highly skilled craftsmen. Some of the best examples of their work are on the **Acropolis** in **Athens**, which contains the **Parthenon** and Temple of Athena (left).

Originally influenced by wooden buildings that had columns made from tree trunks, the Greeks discovered that stone columns could support much more weight. Columns were built from stacks of drum-shaped sections, held together with pegs. These were carved on site, from marble or limestone, and hauled into position by teams of workmen using ropes and pulleys.

The Greeks designed different styles of columns. Doric style columns have plain tops. Ionic columns are thinner with scrolled tops, like on the Temple of Athena.

TEMPLE BOOKENDS

1. Plan out the size of the bookend by positioning the four tubes on the empty foil box, as shown above. If the box and tubes are too long, cut off the extra lengths.

2. Fill the box with gravel and seal up both ends using sticky tape. Use the box as a measure to cut out three pieces of thick card, exactly the same width and length.

3. Cut out four squares from one of the lengths of card. Then do the same with the second length. These squares will make the tops and bases for the columns.

These temple bookends are an elegant and practical way to tidy up any book collection.

Paint the columns to look like real marble.

4. Cover each of the card tubes with the corrugated paper. Cut the paper exactly to size. Then glue it to the tube with the PVA, making sure it is firmly stuck down.

5. Assemble the bookend by gluing four squares of card along the length of the box. Use PVA to glue a column to each square. Make sure each column is secure.

6. Glue another square to the top of each column and finally attach the last card strip to the top. Cover all the flat surfaces with glued pieces of tissue. Then paint the bookend.

15

THE OLYMPIC GAMES

THE OLYMPIC GAMES were held every four years at **Olympia,** in honour of **Zeus.** The first Games date back to 776 BC, but sports competitions had been held amongst rival Greek cities for centuries.

The Greeks admired strength and physical fitness. As most boys were drafted into the army, sports like archery, boxing, fencing, and chariot racing all had a military use and trained the soldiers for war. Successful Olympic athletes were treated as heroes.

This picture painted on a vase in 510 BC shows an athlete holding weights that were used in long jumping.

OLYMPIC PLATE

YOU WILL NEED
Pair of compasses
Thin card
Scissors
Glue stick
Pictures of sports activities

Paper plate
Orange, brown, & black paint
Paint brush
Paper & pencil
Tracing paper

Black felt pen

1. Use a pair of compasses to draw a circle on the card. It will need to be the correct diameter to fit into the centre of the paper plate.

2. Cut out the card circle neatly with scissors. Then paint the circle using the orange paint. Cover the circle evenly with a thick coat.

3. Use the orange and brown paints to paint a border pattern on the paper plate. Let the paint dry, then finish the design with black paint.

4. Choose a sport and draw a design for the centre of the plate on the paper. Either sketch a design or trace a picture from a magazine.

5. Make the design the same diameter as the card circle. When you are happy with the design trace it onto the orange card circle.

6. Follow the lines of the traced design and draw over them with a black felt pen. Then glue the design to the centre of the plate.

Choose scenes from your favourite sports to decorate the plates.

There have been many changes in sports since the first Olympic Games.

PAINTED POTTERY

THE GREEKS WERE MASTER POTTERS and **Athens** was the centre of pot production. Different vase painting styles evolved over the centuries with early vessels having geometric designs.

Then around 720 BC a style known as the 'black figure technique' developed, where figures were painted black against a red clay background. Later, in 500 BC, the process was reversed and 'red figure' vases became the fashion. Many beautiful vases have survived over thousands of years.

Try making some Greek pots from papier mâché. Paint the black-figure and red-figure techniques on different shaped vases.

YOU WILL NEED

Newspaper	Scissors
PVA glue & brush	Cutting mat & craft knife
Balloon	Sticky tape
Card tube	Paper & pencil
Thick card	Paints & brush
Clear varnish	

PAINTED VASE

1. Blow up the balloon. Tear the newspaper into small paper strips. Dilute the PVA glue and use it to cover the balloon with six layers of paper strips.

2. When the paper strips are dry, pop the balloon and remove it. Make the vase shape by taping a section of card tube to the top and bottom, and a circle of thick card to the base.

3. Neaten all the joints by pasting strips of paper across and cover the complete vase with a layer of pasted strips. Roll up a length of newspaper to make the handles.

We can learn so much about the Greeks from the details painted on their pottery, such as the style of their clothing, their armour and weapons.

4. Cut the handles to size and glue them in place, making sure they are secure. Cover them with strips of glued paper, especially where they join the vase.

5. When all the glue is dry, paint the vase white. Now it is ready for painting. You may like to sketch out your design on paper before painting the vase.

Either copy the ideas shown here or look in books about the Greeks. You will find many beautiful examples of painted vases and different shapes to make.

A coat of clear varnish will help to protect your pots.

Vases were painted with pictures of heros, athletes and actors, as well as scenes from everyday life.

TERRACOTTA TOYS

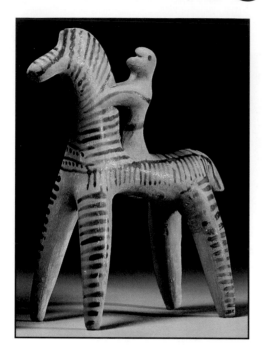

Terracotta toys, like this horse and rider, were found buried in children's graves.

TERRACOTTA HORSE

THE ANCIENT GREEKS were renowned for their sophisticated painted vases and plates (pages 16-18) that were beautifully shaped and decorated. But they also made much simpler forms of pottery. Some date back to the 8th century BC, when the Greek nation started to expand and trade with other **Mediterranean** countries.

Terracotta pots were made to contain oils, perfumes and wine. Simple clay figures and animals were made as toys for children to play with. A Greek clay doll with moving limbs was found with its own small chair and tiny boots.

YOU WILL NEED

Self-hardening clay   Pipe cleaners
Small sponge   Scissors
& water   Paints & brush
Modelling tools   Clear varnish
Newspaper   & brush

1. Look at the shapes of the clay animals opposite. Cut the pipe cleaners to the right length to make a framework for your model.

2. Bend a pipe cleaner to make the body and head shape. Twist lengths of pipe cleaner around the body to make the legs and ears.

3. Cover the work surface with newspaper. Knead some clay in your hands to make it soft. Then start to cover the pipe cleaners with small pieces.

*Try making several terracotta
horses and riders.*

*Make the riders in the same way,
building up the clay over the
pipe cleaner shape.*

4. Build up the horse shape, pressing the clay into the pipe cleaners to make it stick. Keep the clay damp with the wet sponge, as you work.

5. When you have modelled the horse into the right shape, smooth the surface all over using your fingers and the wet sponge.

6. Leave the horse in a safe place to dry. Then paint it with simple patterns. Giving it two coats of clear varnish will help to protect it.

21

GOLDEN TREASURE

Look carefully at the earring above and see the dogs, owls, monkeys and snake that shape the design.

THE GREEKS ADMIRED BEAUTIFUL SCULPTURE, works of art – and beautiful people. But physical beauty was for the wealthy. Men kept their bodies healthy and strong through sport. Rich women wore fine clothes, perfume and gold jewellery.

This golden earring is part of a collection of jewellery called the Aigina Treasure. The treasure was named after the Greek island where it was found. The treasure includes bracelets, brooches and belts. It was made by skilled goldsmiths in about 1700 BC from beaten gold, gold wire and precious stones.

GOLDEN CHARM BRACELET

YOU WILL NEED
Gold poster paint
Gold beads
White tissue paper
PVA glue & brush
Empty sticky tape roll
Gold thread & needle
Scraps of stiff card
Scissors & pencil

1. Brush PVA glue over an area of the empty sticky tape roll, then stick small pieces of white tissue paper to it.

2. Completely cover both sides of the roll with several layers of the glued tissue pieces and leave to dry.

3. Cut out a number of shapes from the card – circles, stars, diamonds, moons. Make a hole in each with the needle.

4. Paint the textured roll with gold poster paint and then paint all the card shapes on both sides.

5. Sew a length of gold thread through each charm. Attach gold beads to the thread and tie each thread to the bracelet.

6. Make some more charms and tie them to a pair of gold earrings so they match the charm bracelet.

Try making a charm bracelet for someone special.

Shape the charms to suit different people by using animal or flower shapes.

GREEK THEATRE

YOU WILL NEED
Pencil & paper
Newspaper
Ruler
PVA glue & brush
Scissors
Craft knife
Modelling clay
Board
Rolling pin
Paints & brush
Thin elastic

GREEK THEATRES were huge outdoor auditoriums. The design of the theatre meant that thousands could see the performance.

Actors also wore thick soled boots and padded costumes to appear larger. Some masks had two faces so an actor could quickly change moods. Other masks had funnel shaped mouths that projected the voice. Male actors played all the roles and clay masks were worn to identify characters.

Expressions were greatly exaggerated on the masks so that they could be seen from a distance.

TRAGIC AND COMIC MASKS

1. First you will need to plan the mask design on paper. Decide whether your mask will be tragic or comic. Make a life-size sketch and draw in all the features.

2. Roll out the modelling clay on the board using the rolling pin. Following your design, roughly model the clay until it takes on the shape and size of your mask design.

3. When the mask is the right size, add more pieces of clay and shape the features. Don't forget that all traditional Greek masks had very exaggerated features.

Make small holes in each side of the mask and thread through the thin elastic so you can wear it or hang it on the wall.

Look at the painting techniques explained on page 9.

4. Tear up a quantity of small strips of newspaper. Use a diluted solution of PVA glue to cover the mould with six layers of paper. Make sure each layer covers evenly.

5. Leave the mask to dry completely, then remove it from the mould. Trim around the mask with scissors and cut out the eyes and mouth holes with a craft knife.

6. Now the mask is ready for painting. Use your imagination to paint it in the colours you think expresses the emotion – whether it's a comic mask or a tragic mask!

BRONZE HELMET

YOUNG GREEK SOLDIERS joined the army at eighteen, but they had to provide their own armour and weapons. Soldiers from wealthy families, that could afford strong metal body armour, became **hoplites**. The well-armed hoplites were a powerful fighting force.

The helmet was the hoplites most important piece of armour. Most Greek designs completely covered the head. They had nose and cheek protectors and small openings for the eyes and mouth. Some bronze helmets had large plumes of coloured horse hair.

This bronze helmet was made in 460 BC and comes from **Olympia**, where it would have been given to the god **Zeus** as an offering.

GREEK HELMET

YOU WILL NEED
Blown-up balloon   Sticky tape
Newspaper   Split pins
Black felt pen   Scissors & string
PVA glue & brush   Bronze & black
Large round bowl   poster paint & brush

1. To make the helmet shape, glue torn newspaper pieces all over the blown-up balloon with PVA glue. Cover with three layers of newspaper.

2. Then cover only the top of the balloon with three more layers of newspaper pieces. Leave the balloon in a safe place to dry and then pop it.

3. Draw the outlines of the eye holes and nose piece on the surface. Cut this shape out using scissors and cut around the base of the helmet.

4. Cut some slits in the sides of the helmet and carefully splay it open – remember the helmet is very thin here! Push the helmet over a large round bowl to keep this curved shape.

5. Tape the helmet to the bowl to keep it firmly in place. Continue gluing a further three layers of newspaper pieces to the bottom part of the helmet covering the slits. Leave to dry.

6. Neaten the bottom of the helmet. Decorate with lengths of glued string and split pins. Cover the ends of the pins inside the helmet with strips of glued paper.

Do not worry if your helmet has some dents – these 'battle scars' will make it look even more realistic!

Paint the helmet with bronze and black poster paints.

STARS OF THE ZODIAC

THE ANCIENT GREEKS had a great love of wisdom. They believed that science and the observation of the stars would give them a greater understanding of the whole universe. Some famous Greek scientists were Pythagorus, Archimedes and **Hippocrates**.

There are 12 constellations in the Zodiac. They circle the Earth each year and your star sign is the one that coincides with your birthday. Above is the constellation of Leo, the lion.

Over 2,000 years ago Greek astronomers identified many star constellations and named them after their **mythological** creatures and heroes. **Ptolemy** listed forty constellations, including Orion and the Great Bear.

ZODIAC CARDS

YOU WILL NEED

Astronomy book with star charts	A4 sheets of coloured card
Drawing paper	Scissors & glue stick
Tracing paper	Paints or felt pens
Pencil & rubber	Gold stars
Ruler	Gold ribbon

1. Fold one of the A4 sheets of card in half to make your card. Draw a 15 mm border on the front of the card. This is the space for the zodiac design.

2. Look through the astronomy book and choose one of the zodiac constellations to draw. Make a sketch of the stars, but make sure your drawing is the correct size to fit on the card.

3. The zodiac constellations are named after a particular creature. Draw the outline of the animal around the stars. Refer to your book as certain stars represent a leg or a tail.

Make one of these unusual Zodiac cards for a friend's birthday.

'Zodiac' comes from the Greek word meaning animal.

4. Take your time over your drawing, don't be afraid to rub out parts and redraw them. When you are happy with it, use the tracing paper to trace it onto the front of the card.

5. You can either colour in your design using the felt pens or paints. Alternatively, cut out the main animal shape from coloured card and decorate it with smaller card shapes.

6. Stick gold stars to the card in the places where the real stars are in the constellation. Finally decorate the border design and glue a gold ribbon onto the front.

TROJAN HORSE

THE LEGEND OF THE WOODEN HORSE tells the story of the Greek army that had besieged the city of **Troy** for ten long years. They were ready to accept defeat, but their leader **Odysseus** had a clever idea.

Trojan soldiers saw that the Greek army had set sail, leaving behind a huge wooden horse.
The Trojans dragged it into the city thinking it was a prize and that the Greek army was defeated.
That night soldiers hidden in the horse opened the gates to the Greek army who had quietly returned and they destroyed the city.

TROJAN GIFT HORSE

YOU WILL NEED

Stiff card
Sharp pencil
Scissors
Ruler
PVA glue & brush
Four drawing pins

Four identical plastic lids
Two 10 cm
dowel lengths
Lolly sticks
Ask an adult to help you
make the wheels.

1. Fold the card in half and draw the simple shape on one side. Cut out the shape, cutting through both thicknesses of card. Be very careful not to cut along the fold.

2. Cut two slits in the top fold of card. Then mark the wheel holes on the folded shape. Pierce through both sides of card with a sharp pencil. Make sure the holes line up.

3. Cut out a piece of card, 8 cm wide, but narrower than the horse. Score and fold it as shown and glue it inside the body of the horse to form the secret compartment.

4. Cut small lengths of lolly stick to size. Glue them to the lids and leave to dry in a safe place. You may need an adult to help you carefully push a drawing pin through the centre of each lid.

5. Decorate the horse's body with glued pieces of lolly stick. Attach a lid to a piece of dowel with a pin. Thread the dowel through the holes, then pin a lid to the other end. Repeat for the second axle.

6. Draw the horse's head on a folded piece of card. Cut out the shape, being careful not to cut along the fold. Decorate the head with pieces of lolly stick and glue it to the body using the PVA glue.

Priam, the Trojan king, ignored the warning, "Fear the Greeks bearing gifts". But why not make a Trojan gift horse and hide a nice surprise inside?

Add small pieces of lolly stick to make a mane and tail, and paint the horse.

MEDUSA AND PERSEUS

MEDUSA was a terrible monster in Greek **mythology**. She had poisonous snakes in her hair and a gaze that turned living things to stone. Perseus was sent to bring her head back.

The Greek gods hated Medusa and decided to help Perseus by giving him special gifts – a polished shield, a **sickle**, a pair of winged sandals, and a helmet that made him invisible. Perseus was able to get close to Medusa without looking at her by using the shield as a mirror. He cut off her head with the sickle.

Medusa's sisters tried to catch Perseus, but he used his magic helmet and winged sandals and flew away unseen.

MEDUSA MIRROR

YOU WILL NEED

Newspaper	Circular mirror
Two large bowls	(without a frame)
(or containers)	Stiff card & ruler
Hot water	Pair of compasses
PVA glue & brush	Craft knife & cutting mat
Paints & brush	String & scissors
	Rubber gloves

1. Make the paper pulp by tearing up small pieces of newspaper into a bowl. Cover the paper pieces with hot water and leave them to soak overnight.

2. Wearing rubber gloves, take handfuls of wet paper, squeeze out the water and put it in the second bowl. Use your hands to mash it together with PVA glue, until it feels soft and smooth.

3. Measure the width of your circular mirror and add 10 cm to the measurement. Then draw a circle of this width onto a sheet of stiff card using the compasses.

*Make sure all
the snakes are dry before
painting them in ghastly colours!*

*Make a hole at the top
of the mirror – and hang it in
the bathroom. Then everyone can
look like Medusa first thing in the morning!*

4. Take your time to carefully cut out the card circle using the craft knife and cutting mat. Glue the mirror to the centre of the card with PVA and leave it in a safe place to dry.

5. Take small lumps of pulp and press them onto the card, building up a textured frame around the mirror. Brush on extra PVA to help the pulp stick to the card.

6. Model lumps of pulp into snake shapes and glue them around the mirror. You may need to let some snakes dry before trying to glue others over the top of them!

THE MINOANS

CRETE is the largest of the Greek islands. It was one of the great centres of culture during the 15th century BC. The **Minoan's** lived on Crete – they were named after the island's king, Minos.

The bull was considered a sacred animal and worshipped by the Minoans. During festivals, offerings were made to the bulls, and acrobats and dancers performed dangerous feats, leaping over the horns of galloping bulls and dancing on their backs.

This clay bull's head was used to sprinkle water as part of a religious ritual during festivals.

MINOTAUR HEAD

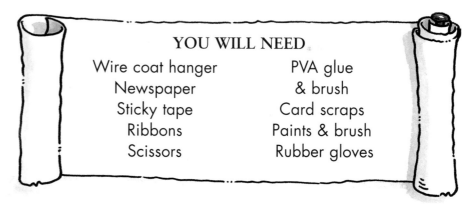

YOU WILL NEED

Wire coat hanger	PVA glue
Newspaper	& brush
Sticky tape	Card scraps
Ribbons	Paints & brush
Scissors	Rubber gloves

1. You will need some help to bend the coat hanger. Twist the sides together, bend them into a curved shape around the hook and bend the hook into a loop.

2. Scrunch several sheets of newspaper together to make a head shape. Add more sheets until the head is the right size and tape them firmly together.

3. Tape the hanger to the back of the head, then cover the wire with strips of paper taped into place. These are the bull's horns, so add paper until they are thick enough.

34

4. Tape two card ear shapes to the head and cover the head with several layers of torn paper, glued with PVA.

5. Smooth over the final layer of paper with your fingers and leave the bull's head in a safe place for the glue to dry.

6. Paint the whole head pale brown and then decorate it with painted patterns. Use the wire hoop to hang the head.

You could hang light-weight objects over the horns or decorate the head with colourful ribbons.

35

CYCLADIC STATUES

THE GREEKS sculpted magnificent bronze and marble statues in honour of their gods and heroes. Sculptors followed strict rules of **proportion** and carved goddess and athletes with beautiful faces and perfect bodies.

But 2,000 years before the age of classical beauty and **realism**, sculptors of the Cycladic Islands in the Aegean Sea carved very simple marble statues to honour their gods. Many figures have been excavated from burial sites or found by divers on the sea bed. All are very similar in their shape, style and simplicity.

CYCLADIC FIGURE

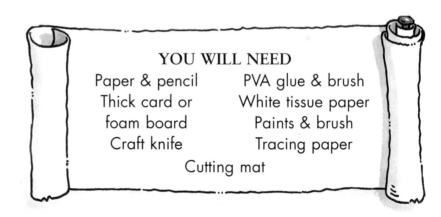

YOU WILL NEED

Paper & pencil	PVA glue & brush
Thick card or	White tissue paper
foam board	Paints & brush
Craft knife	Tracing paper
Cutting mat	

1. Make a sketch of the figure on paper. Look at the examples shown here. Keep the figure very simple. Draw in the nose and arms.

2. Carefully trace the outline of the figure onto the thick card or foam board. Foam board is ideal to use as it is easier to cut out.

3. Now cut out the figure. Make the body and head thicker by cutting out another layer of board and glue these in place with PVA.

4. Cut out shapes for the nose and arms and glue these to the figure. Cut out a square of board for a base. Make a slot in the base for the feet to fit into and glue them in place.

5. Cover the whole figure with small pieces of white tissue, glued with PVA. The tissue will soften the shape and give the figure an interesting texture.

When the glue is dry, paint the figure to look like marble.

Genuine Cycladic figures are priceless, but these models look very convincing!

Cycladic statues are tall, but very thin when looked at from the side.

GLOSSARY

Acropolis – a defensive fort or citadel usually built on the highest point of a city. The hill top acropolis in **Athens** is also where the Athenians built their temples to the gods.

Aristotle – a Greek politician and philosopher who lived between 384 and 322 BC.

Athens – the most important and wealthiest city state in ancient Greece, famed as a centre for art and culture.

Crete – the largest island in the Aegean Sea that formed part of Ancient Greece.

Democracy – a state or country that is ruled by the people where they vote for a leader. This type of government was first utilised in the Greek city states.

Fresco – a large painting decorating walls or ceilings, made by applying paint directly into the wet plaster.

Hippocrates – a Greek doctor who lived between 460 and 377 BC. He believed in treating the whole body and is known as the founder of modern medicine.

Hoplites – well-armed foot soldiers of the Greek army.

Labyrinth – a large maze. The labyrinth on **Crete** was the home of the Minotaur and was impossible to escape from.

Mediterranean – the name given to the sea and the lands and countries surrounding it.

Medusa – a **mythological** creature. One of the Gorgons, it was half woman – half serpent, whose hair was full of writhing snakes and whose gaze turned men to stone.

Minoan – the ancient civilisation on **Crete**. It was named after its king, Minos, and reached its peak between 2200 and 1450 BC.